CEO Guide to Doing Business in Canada

By Ade Asefeso MCIPS MBA

ISBN-13: 978-1499589047

ISBN-10: 1499589042

Publisher: AA Global Sourcing Ltd
Website: http://www.aaglobalsourcing.com

Table of Contents

Disclaimer

This publication is designed to provide competent and reliable information regarding the subject matter covered. However, it is sold with the understanding that the author and publisher are not engaged in rendering professional advice. The authors and publishers specifically disclaim any liability that is incurred from the use or application of contents of this book.

If you purchased this book without a cover you should be aware that this book may have been stolen property and reported as "unsold and destroyed" to the publisher. In this case neither the author nor the publisher has received any payment for this "stripped book."

Dedication

This book is dedicated to the hundreds of thousands of incredible souls in the world who have weathered through the up and down of recent recession.

To my family and friends who seems to have been sent here to teach me something about who I am supposed to be. They have nurtured me, challenged me, and even opposed me…. But at every juncture has taught me!

This book is dedicated to my lovely boys, Thomas, Michael and Karl. Teaching them to manage their finance will give them the lives they deserve. They have taught me more about life, presence, and energy management than anything I have done in my life.

Chapter 1: Introduction

Are you a CEO, consultant, or entrepreneur interested in entering or expanding your business activity in Canadian market?

Then this Book is for you!

The main objective of CEO Guide to Doing Business in Canada is to provide you with basic knowledge about Canada; an overview of its economy, business culture, potential opportunities and an introduction to other relevant issues. Novice exporters, in particular will find it a useful starting point.

Some countries may be subject to export restrictions due to sanctions and embargoes placed on them by the UN or EU. Exporting companies are responsible for checking that their goods can be exported and that they are using the correct licences.

Canada is the second largest country in the world with six time zones, ten provinces and three territories. The capital city of Canada is Ottawa which is located in the province of Ontario. Canada has a population of just under 34 million and 90% live within 200km of the United States border. There are two official languages, English and French. Canada ranks 4th in the world in regards to standard of living (measured according to GDP per capita, e.g. life expectancy, education) which contributes to 'quality of life'. Vancouver, Toronto and Calgary are all within the top five most liveable cities according to the Economic Intelligence Unit (2010).

Canada is an important trade and investment partner for British companies of all sizes and across the spectrum of business activity. Canada is one of the world's richest and most developed countries, ranking among the top ten industrial powers and is recognised as having one of the highest standards of living in the world. With the low inflation and positive economic growth, particularly given the recent global economic crisis, Canada offers good trade and investment opportunities for British companies in many sectors e.g. energy, food and drink, aerospace, biotechnology, financial services, defence & security and business services.

A recent study comparing business costs in Canada, Europe and the USA placed Canada ahead of other G8 countries across a broad range of business operating costs. Canada's market economy has maintained a varied structure with both small companies and multinational companies.

Natural resources remain a major factor, but the growth of hi-tech industries often involving small dynamic companies, is of increasing significance. The proximity of the US market to much of Canada's industrial activity (based largely in Ontario and Quebec) is of fundamental importance to Canada with 75% of Canadian exports going to the USA. This therefore offers UK companies NAFTA access to the US and Mexican market from Canada.

There are also good opportunities for strategic business partnerships and technology transfers between UK and Canadian companies. The market remains receptive to British products and Canadian business are familiar with UK business practices.

Opportunities in Canada

As Canada is not only a natural resources rich country, there are many opportunities across most sectors of this developed and sophisticated market. Sectors include:

- Automotive Energy and power
- Creative and media
- Aerospace
- Pharmaceuticals
- Organic chemicals
- Healthcare
- Mining
- Advanced engineering
- ICT
- Biotechnology
- Financial services
- Defence and Security
- Oil and related products, including environmental technologies

Chapter 2: ICT Opportunities in Canada

In 2008, the ICT sector contributed CAD$60.4B (£39B) to the Canadian economy, 4.9% of GDP, comprised of:

- Telecommunications services 37.3%
- Computer systems & design 24.1%
- ICT manufacturing 14.6%
- Software publishing 7.5%
- ICT wholesaling, rental & leasing 6.4%
- Cable & other programme distribution 6.1%
- ICT services 4%

In 2008, the sector comprised around 32,000 ICT firms and employed 572,700 people, representing 3.3% of overall Canadian employment. Revenues in the sector amounted to CAD$155.3B (£100.2B) and R&D investment CAD$6.06B (£3.9B).

Wireless

At the end of December 2009, there were 22.8million mobile phone subscribers in Canada. Despite Canada's population of 34 million and its vast geography, carriers are able to provide coverage to 99% of Canadians. Canadians send 122 million text messages per day.

The sector will continue to grow due to factors including:

- Comprehensive nation-wide service
- Canada consistently ranks among the top countries offering the lowest customer pricing for wireless services
- Migration from landline to wireless, currently half of all phone connections are wireless
- Mobile data applications (internet, e-mail, telemetry)
- Wi-Fi hotspots continue to increase

The Canadian wireless sector is valued at CAD$36B (£23.2B), with industry strengths including:

- Cellular equipment
- Mobile devices and customer premises equipment (CPE)
- WiMAX
- Ultra-wideband and radio frequency identification
- Software-defined radio (SDR)

Canada is home to global leaders in wireless product and infrastructure developers including Research in Motion (RIM) (wireless solutions for mobile communications), developer of the Blackberry®, Wi-Lan (high speed internet and wireless broadband solutions), Sierra Wireless (wireless data devices).

Wireless industry clusters are present throughout the country, with significant clusters comprising of companies, research centres and universities in British Columbia (Vancouver and Victoria areas), Ontario (Kitchener-Waterloo region, Greater Toronto Area –

GTA, and Ottawa and surrounding area), and Quebec (Montreal and surrounding area).

Software and Computer Services

Canada maintains strengths in design, development, and production of pre-packaged and custom software, including in:

- Enterprise application
- E-Security
- Imaging
- Financial Services

Of the 32,000 ICT companies in Canada, 79% are in software and computer services. Software and computer services industry clusters are present throughout the country, with significant clusters compromising of companies, research centres and universities in British Columbia (Vancouver and Victoria areas), Alberta (Calgary and Edmonton areas), Ontario (Kitchener-Waterloo, Greater Toronto Area – GTA, and Ottawa areas), and Quebec (Montreal area).

ICT Security

Heightened awareness of threats to critical infrastructure such as border crossings, communications, the financial services sector, and to individual privacy and consumer protection has led to increased demand for security solutions.

There are approximately 700 Canadian ICT security companies providing solutions and services related to biometrics, cryptography and encryption, cyber security, ICT security consulting, mobile authentication, public safety, surveillance and tracking technologies.

The majority of these firms are located in and around Ottawa, Toronto, Vancouver and Montreal. The Canadian ICT security market is valued at CAD$1.2 billion10 and projected to reach CAD$2 billion by 2011. SMEs appear to be the drivers to implement ICT security measures, but this tends to be reactive to compliance requirements, such as the Personal Information Protection and Electronics Documents Act (PIPEDA) and the Anti-Terrorism Act (ATA), rather than proactive.

Increased spend is expected to be driven by investment in phishing and pharming solutions, as more and more, hacking activities are done to generate financial gain.

E-Health/Healthcare ICT

Canada Health Infoway is an independent agency whose members include the federal, provincial and territorial Deputy Ministers of Health, and was established to transform and modernise Canada's healthcare system.

Its Vision 2015 outlines the transformation from a paper-based system to an electronic one at a cost of approximately CAD$10 billion, CAD$350 per capita, but with a projected CAD$7 billion per year benefit.

The current cost of healthcare in Canada is CAD$183.1B (£116.8B), approximately 11% of GDP. It is estimated that fully implemented Electronic Health Records (EHR) could produce CAD$6B (£3.9B) in annual savings.

Use of electronic medical/health record (EMR/EHR) varies across the country, with an estimated 23% of Primary Care Physicians adopting the system. Though a number of factors contribute to the low take up, there is a growing trend of patients taking a more proactive role with managing their health.

A number of healthcare organisations have already established online portals geared towards specific patient groups such as diabetics and cancer patients.

Domestic brand awareness remains a challenge for Canadian e-health firms, with some choosing to pursue the US market in lieu of the domestic market (one tenth the size of the US market).

Lack of a national, streamlined system and fragmentation of the Canadian healthcare system makes market penetration difficult as healthcare services are delivered at the provincial/territorial level (13 systems).

The Canadian industry is being encouraged to build brand awareness in order to forge strategic alliances to service the market.

Proven solutions, such as use by the NHS, tend to generate attention for consideration for UK 'IDC: Canadian security market will reach $1B.

Chapter 3: Interactive/Digital Media and Game

The 2008 Canadian Interactive Industry Study estimated there are 2960 interactive/digital media companies in Canada generating CAD$4.7B (£3B) in revenue, with CAD$2.1B (£1.4B) of this generated by the games sector. Around 85% of firms are wholly Canadian owned and the industry employs 51,000-52,500 people.

Canada has over 100 new media programs in professional schools and institutions including the Art Institute of Vancouver, the National Animation and Design Centre, the Banff New Media Institute, and Sheridan Institute of Technology.

Recently, Ryerson University, University of Toronto and the University of Waterloo announced a partnership to create a new digital media programme.

Tax credits, which vary by province, have been a significant factor to enticing interactive media companies, primarily games, such as Electronic Arts, Edios and Ubisoft, to set up operations in Canada.

In addition to tax credits, other factors such as R&D/innovation, related educational institutions/infrastructure generating talent, complementary companies, and domestic and foreign demand, have made Canada an attractive location to maintain operations.

Related financing and new/alternative business models, education and skills development, and attracting and retaining talent, are key issues impacting the sector and areas where the sector is keen to further explore related solutions.

Interactive/digital media clusters are present throughout the country, with significant clusters comprising of companies, research centres and universities in British Columbia (Vancouver and Victoria areas), Ontario (Greater Toronto Area – GTA, and Ottawa areas), and Quebec (Montreal area).

Chapter 4: Photonics Opportunities in Canada

Canada maintains around 370 photonics related companies, employing 20,000 people (40% in R&D) and generates CAD$4.5B (£2.9B) in revenue each year. Annual R&D spend is estimated at around CAD$150M (£97.4M) per year.

International collaboration alliances can be leveraged through R&D and commercialisation opportunities in this market.

Canada is home to world class photonics R&D facilities including the
- Advanced Laser Light Source in Montreal
- TRLabs (ICT consortium) in western Canada
- National Optics Institute in Quebec City.

The province of Ontario maintains about 60% of Canada's photonics industry, with key centres in Toronto, Ottawa, and Waterloo. It also maintains research centres, such as the Centres for Research in Photonics and the Optical Technology Centre, and commercialisation and science parks such as the MaRS Centre, the Life Sciences Technology Park, and the Photonics Fabrication Centre (CPFC), which provides services including simulation, design, fabrication, testing and prototyping.

Much of Quebec's photonics sector is based in and around Quebec City and includes the National Optics

Institute, which has spun off over 20 companies since 1985, along with eight other photonics facilities. British Columbia maintains close R&D/commercialisation links between its three main universities – University of British Columbia, Simon Fraser University and the University of Victoria.

Alberta maintains a number of R&D/collaboration facilities including the National Institute for Nanotechnology (NINT), the Alberta Centre for Advanced Microsystems and Nanotechnology Products (ACAMP) and nanoAlberta.

Chapter 5: Healthcare Opportunities in Canada

Canada has a predominantly publicly financed, privately delivered healthcare system, based on ten provincial and three territorial health insurance plans. The system includes universal, comprehensive coverage for medically necessary hospital, in-patient and out-patient physician services.

Under the Canada Health Act, to receive federal support from Health Canada, provincial/territorial plans must meet five criteria; comprehensiveness, universality, portability, accessibility and public administration.

The healthcare industry is composed of companies involved in the design, establishment, operation, maintenance and improvement of healthcare systems and institutions; telehealth/health telematics; contract research organisations; health administration and consultants; facilities management; continuing medical, nursing and allied health education and training; architectural and design services; clinical services; health insurance.

Over 1.6 million people are employed in the healthcare and social services sector, the third largest employer in Canada with nurses constituting the largest group of health care providers.

Each province has its own unique environment that will influence decisions around health spending. Variations in models of care, salary and benefit levels, health needs and the geographic distribution of a province's population are all factors that can affect health system expenditures.

Public sector funding represents about 79% of healthcare expenditure with the remaining 21% percent financed privately through supplementary insurance and employer-sponsored benefits, or directly through out-of-pocket spending.

In 2008 healthcare spending reached C$172 billion (a 60% increase in 10 years). The healthcare sector contributed significant economic growth amounting to C$79.3 billion or 10% percent of Canada's Gross Domestic Product (GDP) in 2008.

Currently Canada's health care system lists almost 400,000 general practitioners, more than 700 hospitals, and 1,600 long-term care facilities, servicing the population of 33 million.

Opportunities

As the provinces and territories aim to reduce the cost of healthcare, there is demand for equipment and services that reduce the length of hospital stays and recovery times. This includes technology and equipment for non-invasive treatments using sensors, lasers, ultra-sound and nuclear medicine, plus faster and more accurate diagnostic methods and tests.

There is a need for compatibility with existing equipment and long term compatibility, especially with equipment involving PC-linked monitors and telehealth. The use of ICT to deliver healthcare services and information over distances is a growing segment.

Demand is increasing for supplies and equipment for home care, including management of chronic conditions, aids for daily living, and natural, alternative and preventative healthcare products, which help the aging to remain active and independent.

The Canadian Institute for Health Information (CIHI) reports that the home care market in Canada is currently worth about C$6.6-billion, a year. This amount is less than 4% of all the money spent on healthcare.

Drastic changes will have to be adopted and additional support given to this segment of the market to meet the demands of Canada's aging population. Currently 13% of the population is aged 65 or older with a forecasted growth to 25% in the next 20 years.

Overall, Canada remains dependant on imports of medicines, medical devices, imaging equipment and related technology, maintaining a trade deficit of over CAD$10 billion (£5 billion).

The UK's reputation as a source of high quality, innovative products, makes it an ideal supplier to the market. This can be leveraged as an entry point to the US and Mexico, for example, manufacturing in Canada to supply the NAFTA market.

Regulations

Health Canada is the federal government department that oversees the regulation of healthcare components such as pharmaceuticals and medical devices.

Provincial/territorial governments are responsible for delivering healthcare, including licensing of doctors, and building and operating hospitals.

The Therapeutic Products Directorate (TPD), a division of Health Canada, is made up of several Bureau's and is responsible for regulating pharmaceuticals, blood, biologics, disinfectants and medical devices.

The Medical Devices Bureau is responsible for processing license applications, reviewing safety and effectiveness data, and establishing standards and policies.

Medical devices are classified based on risk Class I-V; Class I being the least risky, Class V being most risky.

Characteristics of Canadian Health Market

Medical devices manufactured in Canada include those used for diagnosis and treatment of ailments including medical, surgical and dental equipment, furniture and consumables, orthopaedic appliances, prosthetics and electro-medical equipment, diagnostic kits, reagents and equipment.

Following is a snapshot (most recent figures) of the Devices segment:

- 35,000 employees, representing almost 25% of the total national sector.
- 1,500 corporate facilities across Canada, but primarily based in Ontario, Quebec and BC with over 80% of the device industry based in Ontario and Quebec.
- Device sector is comprised of small, medium and large facilities with the majority of companies in the small to mid-sized area; however, large companies represent 43% of employment.
- Over 600 related importers/distributors.

The industry generates approximately CAD$6 billion (£3 billion) in national sales. Of this, Ontario and Quebec are the largest purchasers; CAD$3 billion (£1.5 billion) and CAD$2 billion (£1 billion) respectively.

In 2008, Canada exported CAD$554 million (£277 million) worth of medical devices (Harmonised System Codes 9022 and 9018) to the USA and CAD$18 million (£9 million) to the UK. In the same year, Canada imported CAD$1.5 billion (£750 million) of medical devices from the US and CAD$46 million (£23 million) from the UK.

Market Trends

Expenditure shifts: Since the mid-1970's, the share of total healthcare expenditure devoted to hospitals, has declined, however, hospitals remain the largest single user of healthcare funds.

In 2008, hospitals made up the largest component of health care spending, drugs accounted for the second-largest share with an estimated annual growth rate of 8.3%, an increase that exceeds other major health-spending categories and Physicians account for the third largest share, a category that has remained stable since 2000.

Expenditure breakdown 2008 (figures rounded): Use of Funds Expenditure (billions) Percentage of total

- Hospitals C$45.5 28.0
- Pharmaceuticals C$30.0 17.4
- Physicians C$21.5 13.4

In its annual report (October 2009) on healthcare spending in Canada, the Canadian Institute for Health Information reports that the country's healthcare spending continues to rise, reaching C$172 billion in 2008 representing 10.1% of GDP. This equates to C$5,170 per person annually.

Delivery

Factors influencing delivery of treatment include expenditure reductions, aging population and new technology. Use of clinics, home care and treatment with medical equipment and drugs, are increasingly incorporated into the system.

Long-term services and follow-up care

These services are now also provided through publicly funded rehabilitation facilities, home care, chronic care institutions and other programmes. Over 270,000 seniors live in healthcare institutions.

The majority of these were newly diagnosed with conditions that often require higher levels of regular care, such as incontinence, stroke, Alzheimer disease or other dementia.

Currently, 1 in 7 Canadians are 65 or older; this number will increase and it is estimated by 2031, 25% of the population will be 65+ accounting for 60% of all hospital costs.

Accessing family physicians

Family doctors are estimated to be in the 98:100,000 population ratio (2007 figure), while the number has increased from 95:100,000 (2001) it is estimated that 5 million of the population are without a family doctor. This ranks Canada last amongst the G8 countries. The Canadian Medical Association (CMA) estimates it will take 26,000 more doctors to bring Canada up to the OECD average.

Nurse Shortages

In 2007, despite the 217,000 registered nurses delivering care; it was estimated that a further 11,000 full time nursing staff are required to enable full service delivery. At the current rate of patient growth, it is estimated that a further 60,000 nurses will be required by 2022.

To counteract some of the shortfall in medical personnel Canada has adopted a plan to 'fast track' medically trained new immigrants through the various compliances and examinations to meet the federal and/or provincial standards to enable quicker introduction into the healthcare sector.

Several Provinces have organized proactive outreach programmes, including fully financed visits for medical professionals, overseas advertising campaigns, and recruitment drives to generate interest in working in Canada.

Private Healthcare

Private-sector (individual) expenditure was forecast to reach C$51.6 billion in 2008 with prescribed drugs and dental care making up the largest components of total private health spending.

Private healthcare is a growing segment and differs in each province:
- In Quebec, British Columbia, Alberta, Prince Edward Island, doctors can set fees and practice outside the public system. Does not

- allow private insurance to cover services provided through private healthcare, which are covered under public insurance.
- Manitoba and Ontario do not allow private insurance, but reimburse doctors who practice outside public healthcare.
- Nova Scotia permits private insurance and healthcare.
- In New Brunswick, doctors can set fees.
- In Saskatchewan, doctors can set fees if they do not practice within public healthcare.
- In Newfoundland, patients can be reimbursed if they utilise private healthcare and use private insurance to cover the difference.

Waiting times are the primary reason for private healthcare demand.

Natural Health and Organic Products

A 2005 Health Canada baseline report reported that 7 in 10 Canadians use Natural Health Products (vitamins/minerals, herbal remedies and teas, additive-free foods and organics).

By 2013 they project that retail sales will be worth CAD$4.75 billion. The Canadian Health Food Association (www.chfa.ca) recognizes NHP is a key component in a healthy lifestyle and as a niche within the Healthcare industry, has growth potential.

The CHFA are working with the Health Products and Food Branch Inspectorate to speed up the tremendous backlog of unprocessed requests for DIN or NPS certification.

Industry Strengths

The Canadian industry has developed strengths including in:

- Cardiovascular - heart valves, pacemakers and catheters
- In-vitro diagnostics - cancer, hepatitis and sexually transmitted diseases
- Radiation therapy and therapy-planning software
- Medical imaging - 3-D imaging, imaging archiving systems and ultrasound scanners and related software
- Dental - high-speed sterilises, dental materials including implants and related equipment and sundries
- Orthopaedics/prosthetics/orthotics - artificial limbs, including myoelectric hands
- Health research - Diabetes Islet Transplant Programme and Human Genome Project.

In addition, Canada maintains strengths in related industries such as biotechnology, advanced materials, microelectronics, photonics, robotics, software and informatics, and telecommunications.

Science/Technology

Many medical device manufacturers collaborate on R&D with universities, hospitals, and government.

About 10% of medical device firms are spin-offs from these collaborations.

Developments in science/technology are an ongoing process it is near impossible to determine those projects that are most important or when a project will come to fruition.

Key Methods of Doing Business

The management and delivery of publicly insured medical services in Canada is the responsibility of each provincial and territorial government. Provinces and territories therefore individually control the planning, management, and financing of hospital care, physician and allied health care services, and some aspects of prescription care and public health.

The 700 publicly financed hospitals account for 75% of medical equipment purchases. The majority of hospitals are part of regional or national not-for-profit buying groups or Group Purchasing Organisations (GPOs). Most hospital goods are either sold direct to GPOs by the manufacturer or through one of the larger importing distributors, mainly based in the provinces of Quebec and Ontario.

Smaller regional distributors tend to supply niche segments and deal with smaller accounts including clinics, smaller hospitals, care homes and doctors' offices. To supply directly to private healthcare is likely to involve sales to each clinic/doctor rather than wholesale distributors.

Factors enabling access to the market include:

- Canada's Mutual Recognition Agreements (MRAs) with the EU, facilitating imports
- Provincial funding initiatives to encourage global partnerships
- R&D tax treatments make it an attractive location for companies to leverage R&D investments
- Joint ventures and strategic partnerships, such as manufacture under private label agreements
- Canada is considered the lowest cost country to establish a medical device firm, with a 4.1 % cost advantage over the US24
- Canada is part of the North American Free Trade Agreement (NAFTA).

UK suppliers opting to serve Canadian customers via US distributors or sales agents should be aware of possible double duties applied to shipments originating from the UK. Direct UK export to Canada is usually the best route to entry.

Chapter 6: Financial Services Opportunities in Canada

Despite the global financial crisis, Canada's financial services industry has remained robust and its overall economy has weathered the downturn well. Canadian banks manage about CAD$3 trillion in assets. In 2010, the finance and insurance sectors contributed CAD$83.5B or 6.7% to Canadian GDP.

Toronto is considered Canada's primary financial services centre and ranked third in the Americas after New York and Chicago. It maintains the ninth largest stock exchange in the world. The March 2011 edition of the Global Financial Centres Index (GFCI) ranked Toronto at 10, Vancouver at 22, and Montreal at 26 among global financial centres.

Public-Private Partnerships (PPP)

The provinces of British Columbia, Ontario, Alberta and Quebec have led Canada's robust PPP project pipeline, primarily within the social and transportation infrastructure sectors, much of which fall to provincial responsibility. The market's steady deal flow, local expertise, and stable economy are among the factors that continue to attract international players across the PPP spectrum.

The mix of foreign and domestic participation has allowed Canada to build up its PPP expertise. Foreign players, including UK companies, have established a presence in Canada to serve the market, including Carillion, Turner & Townsend, Lang O'Rourke, John Laing, Balfour Beatty Capital, Plenary Group, Macquarie. Canadian companies have ramped up their involvement in the PPP market including PCL Constructors, SNC-Lavalin, and Ellis Don. Partnerships between Canadian and foreign players, along with Canada's export driven economy, is leading to interest in new joint export opportunities to third PPP markets, in particular, markets where Canadian companies have an established foot print, such as the US and Latin America.

Financial and Professional Services for Creative and Knowledge Driven Sectors

Canada maintains key strengths in many creative and knowledge driven sectors, however, financing, and development of new business models and revenue streams have not kept pace with supporting these industries.

Significant contribution to the economy and growing sophistication of the film and television industry, interactive media and games sectors, and R&D intensive ICT and Life Sciences sectors have increased demand for related financial and professional services to meet the needs of these sectors.

Chapter 7: Power Opportunities in Canada

Canada is the world's 6th largest energy producer and energy is Canada's second largest industry. In 2009, Canada produced 19.114 quadrillion British Thermal Units (Btu) of total energy.

Canada is a net exporter of oil, natural gas, coal and electricity. It is one of the most important sources for UK energy imports. After China, Canada is the world's second largest producers of hydroelectricity.

Canada has 127.64 gigawatts of installed electricity generating capacity in 2009. The country produced 632 billion kilowatt hours (Bkwh) of electrical power in 2009, while consuming 549 Bkwh (2009). Carbon dioxide emissions from consumption of fossil fuels (million metric tons) is 573.50.

Opportunities

Since 1990, the largest structural change in the production mix has been a decline in hydro power's share of total production (from 63% in 1990 to 60% in 2007). Nuclear power's share has increased recently, as facilities in Ontario returned to service following refurbishment. There have been important increases in combustion turbine generation since 1990 (from <1% in 1990 to 4% today). However, the overall mix masks very considerable regional variations.

In most provinces, generation is either dominated by hydro or by fossil fired thermal although in some such as Ontario there is a more diverse mix. Nuclear plays a key role in Ontario, Quebec, New Brunswick, and potentially Saskatchewan. Hydroelectricity is predominant in British Columbia, Manitoba, Ontario, Quebec, and Newfoundland/Labrador.

Generation, transmission and distribution are provincial responsibilities, so each geographic area will need to be considered as a separate market.

Areas of best opportunity for the UK are:

- Nuclear (Ontario, Quebec, New Brunswick, Saskatchewan)
- Renewables
    - Wind – Canada-wide, but provinces with largest installed wind capacity are Ontario, Quebec, and Alberta
    - Wave/tidal – West Coast and East Coasts (Bay of Fundy has strong potential for tidal energy.) Some potential in Northern Ontario.
    - Solar – Canada wide
    - Sustainable/renewable housing – Canada-wide
    - Conservation initiatives (e.g. smart meters) – Canada-wide
    - Emissions trading – Canada-wide, but centred in Alberta, Quebec and Ontario (as areas of intense manufacturing and energy production). Toronto is the financial capital of Canada.
    - Distributed energy – Canada-wide.

- Biomass – Canada-wide.
- Hydroelectricity – large and small scale.

There is considerable synergy between the UK and Canada in all facets of energy, and it is a sector that welcomes British expertise and innovation.

Chapter 8: Construction Opportunities in Canada

Canada's construction industry continues to experience growth in both residential and non-residential, with an increase in public sector investment continuing into 2012. It represents 12% of Canada's gross domestic product (GDP) when considering its impacts on all sectors of the economy, and it maintains and repairs over $5 trillion in assets.

The Canadian building products sector is directly affected by the level of activity in residential, commercial, industrial and institutional construction/renovation sectors. About two-thirds of the building products consumed in Canada are used in industrial/commercial/institutional construction. The remaining one third is consumed in residential construction.

Characteristics

- One out of 16 workers – about one million - employed in Canada earns a living in this industry.
- Workers are involved in the installation, repair or renovation of $150+ billion of work every year.
- There are over 260,000 firms in the construction industry; 65,000 in residential construction and 150,000 in the trade contracting.

Construction is a pivotal industry across Canada, leading the economy at each turn in the cycle from 2008 to 2012.

Opportunities

In 2013, investment in the non-residential sector is expected to be $339.9 billion, an increase of 5.3% from 2011. Largest increases are expected from Ontario, Quebec and British Columbia.

Capital spending by the public sector will account for nearly two-thirds of the increase. Higher public sector investment is expected to continue in 2014. Capital spending is anticipated to increase 9.9% to nearly $87.8 billion.

Private sector investment is expected to rise 2.8% to $152.2 billion. Significant capital spending increases from the mining and oil/gas extraction sector, as well as the manufacturing sector, are behind that increase.

By investment component, non-residential construction is expected to increase 7.2% to $139.2 billion and account for over three-quarters of total capital spending. More than $2 billion of this increase will come from urban transit projects.
Spending on machinery and equipment is expected to increase by 2.8% to $100.7 billion.

Government Stimulus

Canada's construction industry continues to outperform much of the Canadian economy through the recession period from 2009 to 2012.

In the near term, construction enjoys a soft landing in comparison to the more serious damage inflicted on other industries. Governments' fiscal stimulus is the key driver in 2009 and 2010.

In the 2009 and 2010 construction seasons, close to $5.5 billion was committed to stimulus funding in support of close to 7,000 projects.

All of the funding under the Infrastructure Stimulus Fund was committed. Close to 4,000 projects was approved for construction, accounting for a total investment of almost $10 billion.

Opportunities exist for any innovative construction/building product or green building technology.

Housing Starts

Housing Starts are forecasted to be 185,000 units for 2012, in comparison with 149,000-unit level in 2011. For the seven years, 2002 to 2008 inclusive, annual starts averaged 222,000 units per year.

Top Contractors

The top six Canadian contractors (based on 2009 revenues) are:

1. PCL Family of Companies, Edmonton, Alberta ($6.3 billion)
2. Ellis Don, Mississauga, Ontario ($2.4 billion)
3. Aecon Group Inc., Toronto, Ontario ($2.26 billion)
4. Graham Group Ltd., Calgary, Alberta ($2 billion)
5. Bird Construction, Toronto, Ontario ($882.9 million)
6. Carillion Canada Inc. ($864.5 million)

Green Buildings

Canada is interested in innovative green building technology. In 2004, the Canada Green Building Council adapted the USGBC LEED rating system to the specific concerns and requirements of buildings in Canada. Over 2,000 Canadian projects have registered for LEED certification, from office towers to single family homes. Canadian government requires all of its future buildings to meet LEED's Gold benchmarks.

The LEED Canada Green Building Rating System addresses existing as well as new buildings.

Renovations to residences are focusing on luxurious features, and energy efficiency and more environmentally friendly products (such as energy efficient windows, higher efficiency furnaces, higher efficiency water heaters, lower water consumption toilets, and increased air tightness). Per capita, Canadians are the second higher consumers of water in the world.

Chapter 9: Aerospace Opportunities in Canada

Canada is a major player in the world aerospace industry. It is a world leader in certain key aerospace market segments (such as regional jets, business jets and commercial helicopters) and niche technologies.

The Canadian aerospace sector is export dependent; about 80% of output is exported. It is the nation's leading advanced technology exporter. Some of the industry's small specialist companies lack the necessary resources to react quickly and competitively to today's rapid market changes.

Given Canada's location, the Canadian industry holds a strong position within the US aerospace market (the world's largest market) thus offering an extra dimension to UK suppliers or partners. Along with the United States, Russia, Japan and the European Space Agency, Canada is one of major partners in the International Space Station.

Opportunities

Canada's aerospace industry is the 4th largest in the world. Annual revenues totalled $22.1 (Cdn) billion in 2009. The Canadian industry comprises over 400 companies employing 78,000 employees directly.

Civil applications of aerospace activity accounted for 84.3% ($18.7 billion) of total revenues, with remaining 15.7% ($3.5 billion) associated with military applications. Canada's aerospace industry has several major international firms, including Bell Helicopter Textron, Boeing Canada, Bombardier, CAE, CMC Electronics, GE Canada, Goodrich, Heroux Devtek, Honeywell, L-3 Communications, MacDonald Dettwiler, Magellan, Messier-Dowty, Pratt & Whitney Canada, Rolls Royce Canada and Standard Aero.

Like many industries, it is highly concentrated, with the top 30 firms representing 95 percent of production. Bombardier represents about 45 percent of the industry's sales. Smaller companies, part of the local and global supply chains, round out a significant domestic supply base. Bombardier is building the C Series, a new family of 110-149 seat aircraft.

Leasing companies are seen as the primary customers for this new aircraft. As of July 2010, 90 firm and 90 potential orders were in place.

Bombardier estimates global demand in the 100-to-149 seat market at 6,300 planes, half of which it hopes to capture, as aging fleets are replaced and the CSeries opens up new markets for its customers. The CSeries is on track to enter service at the end of 2013.

The Canadian industry's geographical location allows Canadian companies greater access to the US. The ability to penetrate this aerospace market, the opportunities of which should not be underestimated, could be of further benefit for any potential UK partner or supplier seeking to do business in Canada or the US.

Canada possesses extraordinary world-class capabilities such as:

- Design and production of regional and business aircraft, helicopters, small gas turbine engines, flight simulation systems, landing gears.
- Structural assemblies and components incorporating advanced materials, including composites, special coatings and alloys.
- Avionics, communications, power conversion, environmental controls, in-flight entertainment, and business solutions.
- Maintenance/repair/overhaul of aircraft and major systems and aftermarket logistics support.
- Space robotics, earth observation and communications satellites.

Space

The space sector continued to show growth in 2011 (latest figures available), with total revenues reaching $3.79 billion and employing 6,700 people in 200 companies. This represented an increase of 17.8% over 2010. Export revenues represent 50% of total revenues, with $733M going to the US. European market exports were $399M.

Ontario's proportional share was 72.8% ($2.035B) of total revenues, followed by The Prairies (8.4%), Atlantic Canada (7.2%), Quebec (6.2%), and BC (5.4%).

Amongst the space activities in Canada, the satellite communications sector continued to generate the lion's share of the Canadian space sector's revenues, as it represented 72% of the total space sector revenues with $2 billion in total revenues. Navigation grew to $254M, earth observation reached $200M, robotics increased to $110M, and space sciences decreased to $68M. The top ten highest earning space companies have shown real growth ranging from 12% to 48%.

Along with the United States, Russia, Japan and the European Space Agency, Canada is one of five major partners in the International Space Station.

Major players in the space industry in Canada include: Bristol Aerospace Limited, Canadian Space Agency, Com Dev International, MDA Corporation, Neptec Design Group, Optech Incorporated, and Telesat.

Chapter 10: Public-Private Partnerships Opportunities in Canada

Many Canadian government agencies throughout all levels (municipal, provincial/territorial, federal) have established framework for the use of Public-Private Partnerships (PPP) as an alternative form of financing infrastructure projects.

Canada is experiencing growing populations throughout the country, greater demands on government services and increasing infrastructure gaps with an inadequate tax base to cover requirements.

The infrastructure deficit in Canada is forecast at CAD\$300B (£193.5B) by 2025. The provincial governments, with responsibility for key infrastructure such as hospitals and transportation, are the most proactive in pursuing PPP projects. British Columbia, Alberta, Ontario and Quebec have established related agencies to manage the PPP agenda.

Opportunities

Overall, PPP continues to gain acceptance as an alternative form of financing for all levels of government (municipal, Provincial/territorial, federal) in Canada. Many provincial levels of government have led the momentum and established dedicated

PPP agencies to drive forward the PPP agenda in Canada.

Many UK companies have established a presence in Canada to better service the PPP market, including Carillion Canada, John Laing Infrastructure Canada, Balfour Beatty Capital, Turner & Townsend. Other UK companies are able to serve the market without maintaining a physical presence in Canada.

Federal

The 2007 federal budget outlined a CAD$1.3B (£0.83B) Public-Private Partnerships (P3 Fund) to invest in PPP suitable projects based on the Building Canada Fund. The 2008 federal budget included the establishment of a crown corporation, PPP Canada Inc, to develop and support the PPP market in Canada.

It is meant to facilitate the use of PPP for infrastructure projects throughout the country at all levels, including all projects requesting over CAD$500M (£322.3M) of federal funding will be required to evaluate their suitability as a potential PPP project.

The Agency completed its first call for project applications to the P3 Fund in October 2009. Twenty applications were received from provincial and territorial governments as well as Indian and NAffairs. Six applications were for municipal projects. The projects ranged from CAD$45(£29M) to CAD$500M (£322.3M) in capital costs. PPP

Canada Inc aims to commit over CAD$100M in 2010 (£64.5M) to projects that demonstrate leadership in P3.

Provincial

British Columbia (BC):

Led by the province's PPP agency, Partnerships BC, since its establishment in 2002, 25 projects have been completed, are under construction or have been announced. The investment value of these projects is approximately CAD$10B (£6.4B), CAD$5B (£3.2B) of which is private capital.

British Columbia (BC) is considered the most advanced of the provinces with regard to pursuing PPP projects. Factors supporting the BC model include:

- The establishment of Partnerships BC to foster PPP expertise in the public sector and providing guidance during the procurement process; project assessment, business plan, approval phase, implementation phase. Projects originate from Partnerships BC, which are then presented to BC ministries for consideration.
- Use of the Capital Asset Management Framework (CAMF) to assess traditional versus alternative means of financing projects.
- Maintaining a balance between the public's right to know versus protecting the private sector's intellectual property.

- Commitment to the use of PPP; 10-20% of capital projects are expected to use PPP.

Alberta:

Alberta has established the Alternative Capital Financing Office (based within the Alberta Treasury Board) to assess the use of alternative means, including PPP, in pursuing capital projects where better value can be demonstrated.

The province's 2010-13 Capital Plan outlines plans for CAD $20B (£12.9B) worth of capital projects for municipal infrastructure, highways, healthcare, schools, community facilities, water and wastewater management, housing, government facilities, equipment and other capital.

PPP projects pursued in the province include the Anthony Henday Southeast ring road in Edmonton, the Northeast Stoney Trail ring road in Calgary, and the Alberta Schools Alternative Procurement project (ASAP). In June 2010, 18 new schools were built using the PPP.

These schools were completed a month ahead of schedule and it is estimated that the province saved CAD$97B (£62.3M) compared to the cost had the schools been built using traditional methods. The second phase of 14 new P3 schools is currently under construction and is due to be completed in 2012-13.

The Province does received substantial royalties from the oil and gas sector and is the only province without a provincial sales tax. However, infrastructure demands have not kept pace with Alberta's recent and rapid economic expansion.

Ontario:

In 2004, the Ontario Ministry of Public Infrastructure Renewal (MPIR) released its framework strategy for Alternative Financing and Procurement (AFP), 'Building a Better Tomorrow' and in 2005, established Infrastructure Ontario, a branch of MPIR. This framework follows similar to that of BC in terms of approving PPP/AFP projects encompassing appropriate risk transfer and visible value for money under a system of transparency and accountability.

The Ontario government outlines priorities and outcome objectives. Infrastructure Ontario is tasked with determining which method of procurement to utilise; PPP and non-PPP options.

The ReNew Ontario: Five-Year Infrastructure Investment Plan includes CAD$30B (£19.4B) worth of infrastructure investment. About one-quarter of these projects will be AFP.

There are 40 AFP projects currently in the pipeline for development, most in the healthcare sector. Of these One-quarter valued between CAD$50M (£32.3M) and one-half valued between CAD$100M (£64.5M). Ontario's infrastructure gap is estimated to be over CAD$100B (£64.5B).

Quebec:

In 2010, Infrastructure Québec was established to oversee all provincial government infrastructure procurement and construction in Quebec. It will consider how projects are procured and assumes the role of the former L'Agence des partenariats public-privé du Québec (PPP Quebec).

Municipal

More and more, municipal levels of governments are taking up the use of PPP. Their limited resources, capacity and internal expertise in this field has lagged from the pace of provincial level of government using PPP. There are a number of municipalities that are now actively pursuing a PPP agenda, including the cities of Ottawa, Winnipeg, and Calgary.

Outlook and Market Access

With the majority of responsibility for infrastructure development at the provincial level, the pace of PPP progress will continue to differ across the country. However, governments are seeking new solutions to meet infrastructure demands and overall, PPP is gaining momentum as a viable alternative. The federal government has recognised this and has established a federal government agency, PPP Canada Inc, to better co-ordinate efforts across the country.

Provincial government agencies recognise domestic capacity is being strained to fulfil the current PPP pipeline, with many PPP project tenders seeing similar bidders shortlisted partly due to limited domestic PPP expertise. These governments are encouraging more international bidders/consortium partners on projects in order to ease the pressure on domestic capacity, and introduce more innovation and competition in the market for PPP projects.

Certain restrictions exist to direct market access by foreign firms such as practising law, some government tenders may require local partners, differing levels of government support for PPP, etc. However, factors such as a similar legal system to the UK, language, longstanding Canada/UK historical, cultural and business relationships, skilled workforce, etc, give rise to opportunities for UK firms in the Canadian PPP market.

The UK financial and related professional services industries are well regarded in Canada. Canadian industry is keen to partner with British players to create win-win business relationships. UK firms with PPP expertise are winning business in the Canadian market, either directly or with Canadian partners.

Opportunities for UK firms include:
- Direct bidding on government tenders. PPP tenders can be viewed on related provincial PPP agency sites or on Merx www.merx.com, a central procurement portal utilised by all levels of government to post public tenders. Some exceptions apply to listing, for example, on Merx, value of the tender, sensitive nature of software/technology required,

emergencies, etc. In these instances, the agency will manage the tender directly.

- Providing guidance to Canadian governments at all levels and the private sector on the PPP process. The UK's experience and expertise in this field lends well to Canada's developing PPP industry. The market welcomes and is keen to understand lessons learned from the UK. Though Canada maintains a highly skilled workforce, UK expertise can fill the knowledge gap in order to strengthen the PPP skills set of the Canadian market.

- Canadian firms have ready and direct access to the market. UK firms can leverage this advantage to partner with firms interested in pursuing PPP projects. Though progress on PPP may differ among governments, the private sector is eager to pursue opportunities in this field and develop its expertise.

- Many Canadian companies have established business relationships with other markets such as the US and South America. Once partnerships in the Canadian market are established, there may be potential for Canada/UK partnerships to pursue PPP projects in third markets.

Chapter 11: Biotechnology/Pharmaceutical Opportunities in Canada

Canada maintains 668 biotechnology firms, considered second in the world in terms of number of companies. Ninety percent are SMEs and generate 4% of global biotech revenues.

Firms present across the country, including Western Canada (Alberta, British Columbia) 38%, Ontario 26%, Quebec 20%, Atlantic (New Brunswick, Newfoundland, Prince Edward Island) 10%, Prairies (Saskatchewan, Manitoba) 6%.

In 2009, spending on prescription drugs amounted to CAD$25.4B (£16.4B) and non-prescription drugs amounted to CAD$4.6B (£3B), an overall increase of 5.1% from 2009.

It is estimated that 54% of prescription drugs purchased was generic drugs.

Opportunities

A concerted effort by academia, industry, government, associations and the financial community has helped Canada become a world leader in biotechnology. Canadian companies and research organisations are attractive international business partners as the country is well-placed to provide access to other NAFTA markets. Canada currently has 301 health biotech products in the pipeline and 60 therapeutic medicines on the Canadian market as a result of R&D in Canada.

UK firms GSK and AstraZeneca maintain significant presence in Canada. In 2007, GSK invested CAD$178M (£116M) in R&D and maintains facilities in Quebec, Ontario, Alberta, British Columbia and Nova Scotia. AstraZeneca maintains operations in Ontario and an R&D centre in Quebec and invests CAD$2M (£1.3M) per week on research.

R&D and Technology Transfer

Canada has recognised that strong scientific expertise and continuous investment in R&D are key factors to growth in the industry. Governments at all levels have invested in a supportive infrastructure for the industry.

Canadian firms have strong linkages with leading research and academic institutions and access to public funding opportunities for research conducted in Canada. Partnerships between UK and Canadian firms and academic institutions can be used to leverage these opportunities.

In 2007, R&D spend amounted to CAD$1.3B (£0.84B). The research community is comprised of approximately 30,000 people based from 17 medical schools and more than 100 teaching hospitals. In addition, a series of funding programmes and tax credits offer support for the industry.

Some examples are noted below

In 1983, the federal government developed a national biotechnology strategy and established the National Research Council's biotechnology programme. The strategy set out to stimulate the development of a critical mass of research infrastructure, large pools of post-graduate and post-doctoral research, world-class academic, public and private sector research investigators, entrepreneurs and a biotech sector vision. Established in 1992, The Networks of Centres of Excellence (NCE) programme links academic and industry researchers. Since 1994, the nine biotechnology NCEs have spun-out 40 new companies to commercialise technologies. The federal government provides CAD$77.4M (£50M) of funding each year. The Scientific Research and Experimental Development (SR&ED) programme is a federal initiative offered to Canadian controlled firms pursing scientific research. Firms can apply to tax credits against wages, materials, machinery, equipment, some overhead, and SR&ED contracts. These firms can claim a tax credit of 35% up to the first CAD$2M (£1.3M) of qualifying expenditure, and 20% of any excess. Research must be undertaken in Canada.

In May 2010 the government announced the first group of 20 Canada Excellence Research Chairs. This programme awards up to CAD$10M (£6.5M) over seven years to each chair holder and their research team. One of the four priority research areas for this programme is health and related life sciences.

Chapter 12: Non-Health Opportunities in Canada

Non-health Opportunities in non-health biotech also exist predominantly in agri-bio applications such as food and crop sciences, marine, environmental bio-applications and renewable energy.

There are currently 216 companies in the field of industrial and environmental biotechnology engaged in efforts of advanced manufacturing, alternative energy and sustainable biomaterials.

There are currently 165 companies engaged in agriculture biotechnology. Industry Clusters Biotechnology and pharmaceutical clusters are found throughout the country. Key hubs include:

Ontario

Industry strengths include bioinformatics, genomics, biomaterials, biomedical engineering, stem cells and regenerative medicines, drug discovery, medical devices, agricultural biotechnology, bio-products, functional foods and nutraceuticals.

The province has more numerous renowned research centres and researchers, including the MaRS Discovery District in Toronto and The National Research Council (headquartered in Ottawa with branches throughout the country). Established in 2000, MaRS fosters commercialisation from scientific innovation. MaRS is a partnership between universities, hospital researchers, business and finance. It is also home to the Ontario Genomics Institute.

Quebec

Industry strengths include genomics, biopharmaceuticals, bioinformatics, medical technologies, manufacturing, clinical research, and hosts research institutes such as Genome Quebec Innovation Centre and McGill University.

In 2008, the province announced the creation of a public-private consortium in order to accelerate drug development, and develop safer and more effective drugs. The Consortium for Drug Discovery consists of an alliance between federal and Quebec government agencies, and Pfizer Canada,

British Columbia

Industry strengths include biopharmaceutical and biomedical. Support infrastructure includes the University of British Columbia, the BC Cancer Agency, and the BC Centres for Disease Control.

Other clusters

Canada's vast and differing geography has also influenced the biotech industry. Agri-bio clusters are located in the Prairie Provinces (Alberta, Saskatchewan, Manitoba), while aquaculture and marine sciences clusters are located in Atlantic Canada and the Pacific coast of British Columbia.

Chapter 13: Food and Drink Opportunities in Canada

Canada's market for food and beverages is estimated to be worth C$187.7 billion; in category percentages: meat/poultry 24%, dairy 14%, beverages 11%, baked goods 9% and processed fruit/vegetables 9%; the remaining 33% represents pet foods, grain/oilseed milling, sugar/confectionery, seafood and other speciality foods.

Foodservice/hospitality account for approximately C$58 billion Imports account for approximately 23% of the market and equally 23% is attributed to exports. The USA continues to hold its position as Canada's main supplier and buyer.

The market is dominated, in most sectors, by multinationals, some of whom have established manufacturing/processing in market, e.g. Kraft, Nestle, Cadbury and Baxter's.

Food imports from the UK in 2008 amounted to approximately C$220 million. On average Canadians spent 11.3% of their personal consumption expenditure on retail food purchases.

The Canadian alcoholic beverage industry is estimated to be worth over C$20 billion. UK alcohol exports to Canada amounted to approx. C$189 million in 2008. On average the sale of alcohol beverages is on the increase due in part to a shift in demographics (baby boomers) and their interest in better quality premium beverages. Beer continues as the alcoholic beverage of choice in Canada at 52.2% (of legal age) per capita consumption; about 80%. Euro monitor predicts moderate growth within the sector.

The UK is a well-established supplier to the Canadian market and enjoys an on-going reputation for producing high quality innovative products and attractive packaging. Because almost 25% of the population of Canada is either British, of British descent, or of Commonwealth extractions, there is a built-in knowledge of, and loyalty towards, British brands and confidence in British food and beverage products.

The current global economic downturn has had impact on the cost of food and beverages, without exception. Key factors are the cost of fuel, energy and ingredient prices plus currency exchange rates. Fuel costs ultimately increase transportation costs and as Canada relies heavily on food imports, particularly fresh produce, during the winter months this has had a significant effect.

Typical ingredients travel at least 1,500 miles. There is, however, a small but growing trend towards sourcing locally grown and prepared foods, and this is likely to develop as consumers embrace ways of improving their lifestyle and eating habits, reducing waste and their individual environmental impact.

Opportunities

Today's economic downturn is causing consumers to 'watch their pennies' in many areas of their lives. Many consumers are trading down to find affordable food/beverage options; shopping in discount retailers, buying lower value private label brands, bulk shopping, taking advantage of sales/discounts and preparing more stay at home meals.

The Private Label market in Canada is estimated to be worth almost C$11 billion and supermarkets are heavily promoting private label as an affordable alternative to national brands. National brands are valued at C$46 billion and according to Neilsen Market Track is maintaining growth rate, but not gaining ground. The industry has adopted a new term 'shift to thrift'.

One area of the food sector that seems to be unaffected is the natural and organic segment. Health Canada's baseline study in 2005 suggested that 7 in 10 Canadians use natural health products (vitamins/minerals, herbal remedies and teas, additive-free foods and organics). Consumption of organics is about 1-2% of total food consumption but it is a growth area at about 20% per annum. Canada introduced its own organic standards and regulations in June 2009; this should in turn bring about greater consumer confidence and a further lift in consumption.

Natural products, once only found in health food stores, have found their way into main stream grocery and supermarkets thus meeting the increased demand of consumers who continue to explore healthier alternatives in their daily diets.

Digestive health (probiotics and prebiotics), antioxidants and weight management coupled with preservative-free products (additives, artificial colours/flavours, fats, sugars and sodium), and whole grains are a key growth area as **are Kosher and Halal foods**, which are sought out by mainstream consumers because of their perceived health benefits. According to a spokesperson with the Halal Monitoring Authority in Toronto there are minimal choices of halal-certified products available for Canada's 1 million Muslims.

To counteract the lack of choice many Muslims resort to kosher-certified foods, both segments are well positioned for growth in the near future. Other segments unaffected by the current recession are baby/infant and pet foods

Other categories that offer current opportunities include:

Baking Aids, Couscous, Instant Breakfasts, Toaster Pastries, Coffee Creamers, Rice Drinks, Snack Foods, single serve confectionery/chocolate, Infant/Toddler Snacks, Energy Drinks, Bagged Vegetables/Salads, Canned Vegetables, Stuffing Mixes, Cake Decor, Canned Ice Tea, Cocktail Mixes.

Alcoholic Beverages

The Canadian industry has shown tremendous growth over the past 6 years with UK companies being well positioned to take advantage of continuing trends in key areas such as speciality beers, single malts and deluxe spirits. The UK exported approx C$189 million in 2008.

UK companies have achieved success with most liquor commission in Canada, however, The Liquor Control Board of Ontario (LCBO) aside from being the largest of the provincial liquor commission (604 outlets), has been the most active in showcasing and listing British products.

The LCBO has established itself as an effective merchandiser with programmes aimed at educating its customers with tastings, cooking demos, shelf flyers and a high quality (complimentary) monthly magazine. The LCBO's total net sales in 2007-08 amounted to C$4.1 billion. The UK was 2nd in the spirits category with net sales of C$208 million.

Knowledge and developed tastes among consumers, for wines, high-end spirits (including single malts) and speciality beers will continue and will ensure growth in these sectors. The UK is well positioned to serve most of these categories.

Market Size

Total sales within the food industry were estimated to be worth approximately C$91 billion. Large supermarket and independent grocery chains account for approximately C$79 billion, with the balance attributed to mass merchandisers C$4 billion) warehouse clubs (C$5 billion) drugstores (C$2 billion) and speciality stores and non-traditional outlets (C$1 billion). Canadian Grocer magazine predicts an increase of 3.1% in 2012, despite the economic downturn, based on the industry maintaining a high level of special promotions. 2008 saw the lowest consumer expenditure on food/beverages in recorded history at 8.51% of total expenditure (down from 9.45% in 2001).

The foodservice industry accounted for sales of approximately C$57.5 billion in 2007 generated via full service restaurants, fast food outlets, hotels, hospitals, recreational facilities, and vending machines. This segment of the industry is experiencing a downturn as the consumer, feeling the economic pinch, reverts to home cooking. The Canadian Restaurant and Foodservices Association, however, are predicting a recovery in 2013.

Trends in Market

The Canadian food industry, particularly supermarkets and grocery chains, looks to the UK as an innovator and leader in the development and marketing of private label or store brands. This is an area that continues to be a force within the industry. Many of the large food retailers have remodelled and expanded their stores to include non-food items, such as pharmacy/health/beauty boutiques, photo services, etc.

Likewise non-traditional food outlets, such as drugstores, mega-retailers, and gas bars are expanding their food/beverage ranges.

The UK is highly regarded as a supplier of quality high-value confectionery, preserves, teas and biscuits. While many of these products, especially the well known global brands, are found on supermarket shelves, they more frequently are available in smaller speciality and gourmet food stores, whose clientele tend to be well travelled, knowledgeable about UK brands and with a larger disposable income.

Confectionery continues to sell well. Speciality stores look to supply their customers with quality and attractively packaged products and while consumers buy reduced quantities of confectionery; their purchases tend to be more expensive. The rise in Type 2 diabetes and an increased rate of obesity has adults looking to downsize their confectionery 'treats' rather than eliminating them altogether. Opportunities exist for manufacturers producing single-serve and bite size confectionery and premium chocolate.

Tea consumption continues to grow, fuelled by its perceived health benefits. Nine out of ten Canadians drink tea. There is a rising demand for speciality teas including high-end blends, herbal/fruit, iced (powders and liquids) and green teas. The number of 'coffee shop' retailers has risen sharply, most are franchise businesses that serve and retail their own private-label lines. It is estimated that at least 30% of all coffee is consumed in restaurants and coffee shops with the average coffee drinker consuming 2.828 cups per day. Overall, the tea and coffee market is worth about C$368 million.

The non-alcoholic beverage sector represents a large category within grocery stores. The growth trends have been in the following categories:
- chilled juices,
- nectars,
- iced teas,
- soya drinks and the ever-popular soda pops.

The future trend is however towards energy drinks/nutraceutical blends, which offer built in vitamins and minerals. However, as Canada regulates the sale of these products, the growth of the sector may not be immediately visible.

The market for high quality 'ethnic' products, such as Mediterranean and Mexican, and those that crossover into the mainstream food market are currently very popular and offer potential growth. Indian food continues to see steady growth particularly in ready meals, breads and accompaniments.

Nielsen's Market Track recorded total sales of Indian food brands in 2008 to be valued at C$27 million, up 15% from 2007.

Of continuing importance and highlighted for steady growth are the high-quality functional and nutritional foods that appeal to the growing demand for tasty, natural and safe foods. This 'category' includes food and beverage products enhanced with probiotics, omega fats, fibre, antioxidants, calcium, vitamins etc.

Currently this market segment is estimated to be worth C$6.6 billion with a per capita spend of approximately C$212 and every indication of rapid growth. Canada's institutions and research facilities are well positioned to partner with UK companies to develop new and diverse products.

The organic market continues to show steady growth and is estimated to be worth C$1 billion. Supermarkets sold C$412 million (£206 million) worth of certified organic food in 2006, a 26% increase over 2005, representing 41% of total organic foods sales in Canada. Consumers are purchasing organics for their perceived health benefits and in support of sustainable agriculture, a trend that can only grow as scientific evidence proves the benefits of organic consumption.

As consumers become more environmentally conscious there will be further demand for food and beverage products to be packaged in biodegradable, recyclable or re-usable packaging. Consumers will want evidence that a manufacturer is 'green' and environmentally friendly. Supermarkets and retailers in general are encouraging customers to use re-usable shopping bags and charging fees for plastic bags.

One of the main overriding drivers of trends in the market in Canada is the ever changing demographics that includes the age-related shopper (boomers, gen x and y), shifting immigration patterns, and economic factors as they pertain to the 'have and have-nots'.

Constraints, Regulations and Standards

Meat and Poultry

Meat Inspection Act and Regulations and the Export and Import Permits Act

Before products are imported into Canada, the exporting country must be evaluated by the Canadian Food Inspection Agency. The country must prove that they have a national meat inspection system, including a residue monitoring programme, equivalent to that of Canada. Also, the Canadian Food Inspection Agency must inspect and approve individual foreign manufacturing and processing companies before they are eligible to export their products to Canada.

Dairy Products

Agricultural Products Act

Butter, Cheddar Cheese, dry milk products and variety cheeses are regulated by the above Act. Each shipment must be accompanied by an Import Declaration and is subject to Import Control (Quota).

Cheese and other dairy products are controlled under a Quotation System. Quotas are given to Canadian companies, and only those importers/distributors/retailers holding quota are able to import dairy products.

The Meat and Dairy sectors are of particular importance to British producers, but there are also many other Acts and Regulations that govern the importation of food products into Canada.

UK companies requiring further information should contact The Canadian Food Inspection Agency to obtain their "Guide to Importing Food Commercially".

Labelling

Food and Drug Act and Regulations and the Consumer Packaging and Labelling Act and Regulations

All food packaged for consumer use and imported into Canada must comply with basic food labelling requirements. Labelling requirements include the common name of the food, a list of ingredients and components, the name and address of the responsible party, a net quantity declaration in metric and a "best before" date when required. Nutritional labelling is mandatory on pre-packaged goods, with few exceptions. The package must include a standard nutritional box with a detailed breakdown of contents based on a serving size.

The format and information provided must comply with the Guidelines on Nutritional Labelling developed by Health Canada. All mandatory labelling information and nutritional labelling, other than the name and address of responsible party, is required to be declared in both French and English.

Additional information on labelling is available from Canadian Food Inspection Agency.

Natural Health Products Directorate

This department is part of Health Canada's Health Products and Food Branch. It is responsible for setting new rules and regulations to govern the sale of natural health products. All products will be classified as either a food or a drug, the latter of which will require a Drug ID Number. Products are required to carry clear identification and instructions for use, warnings and cautions.

Product Codes

Product codes are not regulated by government, but rather administered by the not-for-profit standards council GS1 Canada (formerly the Electronic Commerce Council of Canada). Until 2005 retailers required that the food merchandise they carry, other than alcoholic beverages, be labelled with a Universal Product Code (UPC), a 12 digit machine-readable code that identifies a consumer package. However, GS1 Canada agreed to 2005 Sunrise, an agreement designed to ease trade restrictions between Europe and North America. As a result, Canadian retailers can also scan and process European Article Number (EAN) codes. The new Data Bar-code is being tested in some Canadian supermarkets, while it will not replace the UPC code it is becoming very popular as it can store more information and can be used successfully on loose produce (fresh vegetables and fruit).

For more information concerning product codes contact GS1 Canada (www.gs1ca.org)

Alcoholic Beverages

Market Size

The sale of alcoholic beverages in Canada is controlled by Provincially-managed monopolies and licensing systems. Each Provincial Commission or Board has its own set of rules/regulations that govern the purchasing, sale and distribution in their respective jurisdiction. The provincial systems should not, however, be considered a deterrent to doing business in market.

The alcoholic beverage market in Canada is estimated to be worth $20 billion. The Canadian industry has shown tremendous growth over the past 6 years with UK companies being well positioned to take advantage of continuing trends in key areas such as speciality beers, single malts and deluxe spirits. The UK exported approx C$189 million in 2008.

The western provinces of Alberta, British Columbia and Saskatchewan have just announced the creation of a partnership designed to strengthen interprovincial and cross border trade. This could have a very positive benefit to the alcohol beverage industry in the West as it may lead to streamlined liquor distribution and regulations. Business opportunities as a result of this partnership will become apparent in the near future.

Trends in Market

Consumers have developed tastes and are very knowledgeable about alcoholic beverages, a fact reflected in the steadily increasing demand for imported wines and high-end spirits.

These categories continue to grow and are much less price-sensitive than imported beers. Prepared alcoholic beverages (RTD's and coolers) are growing in popularity as they appeal to new consumers and those interested in trying something innovative whilst still enjoying their favourite flavours.

Canada is considered a 'nation of beer drinkers'; the market is dominated by a small number of global and North American companies. There is a quickly growing market for cheap "no frills" beer, which is comparable to standard domestic products but is retailed for a considerably cheaper price. This has pushed low-end domestic brands to reduce their prices in order to compete, and helped push a number of companies into mergers. Despite this, there continues to be a steady market for darker, tastier beers produced by the craft or microbreweries.

Food

The appointment of a local distributor, who acts either as an importer or works in connection with a national broker, is usually the best way to enter the market. Canada is a very large country and to ensure complete coverage it is necessary to appoint a distributor who has representation nation-wide, via a team of sales representatives and warehouses.

Supermarkets and grocery chains, in some cases, will buy directly from manufacturers; however they usually stipulate that the supplier must have current sales experience in dealing with UK supermarkets.

Many speciality food products are sold, on an exclusive basis, directly to independent food retailers, who specialise in the niche gourmet market.

Trade shows are an effective avenue for launching new product lines, as distributors and agents take advantage of the many annual shows nation-wide and in the USA and Europe.

Many supermarkets and chains provide opportunities for in-store tastings. Direct marketing campaigns, flyer advertising, discount coupons, and giveaway deals are all used in marketing and advertising campaigns.

E-Commerce as a method of selling groceries via Internet shopping is surviving in larger urban areas. It remains to be seen whether consumers will continue to support this method of grocery shopping, and it is unlikely to impact on traditional shopping.

The best method of approaching this very competitive market is through the appointment of a local agent or representative. Many of the large agencies have offices/representatives in all of the major regions across the country. However, smaller agencies may only work within one region, if this is the case, it may be prudent to investigate the appointment of several different regional agents.

Constraints, Regulations and Standards

Canadian provincial government liquor boards have exclusive control over Canada's alcoholic beverage retail pricing, listings, distribution and sales in most provinces. Alberta is the only province that has deregulated the sale and distribution of alcoholic beverages.

British Columbia started the process of deregulation in January 2003, but the project is currently on hold. Each province should be viewed as a separate market, as some regulations and requirements may differ between liquor boards.

Canadian Standard Product Code (CSPC)

The Canadian Standard Product Code is a six digit numeric code preceded by a "+" sign, used to universally identify alcoholic beverages marketed in Canada. Provincial liquor control boards require that the CSPC be used on all individual bottles and cartons over 100 ml in size.

It is recommended that companies seek guidance from the individual liquor boards with regard to use of product codes.

The Liquor Boards are all-different and operate independent of one another. Obtaining a permanent listing for a beverage is the ultimate goal, however, shelf space is limited and not every supplier or product is viable. There are year round time-limited presentations of products, usually by type (beer, whisky) and depending on consumer response a product may be invited back with a permanent listing. Consumers and the hospitality sector may also take advantage of placing private orders thus providing opportunities for connoisseurs or restaurants to have exclusivity on particular brands/lines.

Chapter 14: Canada Economic Overview

The UK is Canada's second largest partner worldwide in the science and technology sector, with a particularly close relationship in the field of clinical research. Canada sees itself as a world leader in scientific discovery, and it has strong energy, mining, ICT, and bio-sciences sectors.

The province of Ontario holds North America's 3rd largest biotechnology cluster and has been named one of the top five regions in North America targeting biotechnology companies in 2009. In Ontario alone, the life science sector employs more than 43,000 people at approximately 850 companies and generates $14 billion in revenues annually.

Canada has the second highest number of research publications coming out of the University of Toronto, only outnumbered by Harvard University in the US. Canada also has strengths in various areas of Information technology, engineering, and clean technologies. Particular energy strengths include the oil sands, wind energy, carbon capture and storage, and biomass sectors.

Marine energy (primarily tidal or wave turbines) and bio fuel sectors are expected to gain prominence in the commercial sector within five to seven years.

The UK and Canada share deep cultural and historical ties, with broadly similar legal and political systems.

The UK is Canada's primary European trading partner. Canada is the UK's 16th largest market, with exports reaching £3.25bn in 2008. The UK is also the second largest foreign direct investor in Canada after the US. Canada is the UK's third largest export market outside Europe, the US and China. The value of UK goods exported to Canada totalled approximately £3.6 billion in 2008. Energy products, industrial goods and machinery products dominated UK goods exported to Canada in 2008. Between January-May 2009 the value of UK exports were £1.5 billion.

Canada emerged from the recession with modest growth in September 2009. As the Canadian dollar continues to strengthen, the composition of GDP has shifted away from net exports and towards final domestic demand. With slow growth and risk from a strong Canadian dollar, Bank of Canada maintains commitment to hold interest rates at 0.25% (from 4.25% a year ago) through the second quarter of 2010.

Unemployment is easing (8.5%); with public sector accounting for over half the new job gains. The Bank of Canada expects growth to pick up as consumer spending and business investment begins to increase. Canada and the EU started a round of Free Trade talks in September 2009 with the expectation of a final deal at the end of 2012. Both the EU and Canada are looking for a positive outcome to these talks which could open up the market for both sides. For example, both sides could open up their markets with the removal of quotas or non tariff barriers on agricultural, including dairy, products.

Both sides have said that they are in 90% agreement, but the final 10% of both sides concerns will be where most of the work will be in the talks during 2012. From the EU side, the main priorities remain Intellectual Property protection in Canada and access to Canadian Government Procurement at a Federal and Provincial level.

Chapter 15: Canada Political Overview

Population

In October 2009 Canada's population was estimated at 33 million. Principal population of metropolitan areas:

Calgary (Alberta) - 1.1 million Edmonton (Alberta) - 1.1 million Halifax (Nova Scotia) - 394,000 Montreal (Quebec) - 3.7 million Ottawa (Ontario) - 1.1 million Toronto (Ontario) - 5.5 million Quebec City (Quebec) - 700 thousand Vancouver (British Columbia) - 2.2 million Victoria (British Columbia) – 348,000 Source: Statistics Canada, 2008.

Canada was established in 1867 as a self-governing Dominion within the British Empire and attained full sovereignty in 1931 (Newfoundland joined later in 1949). With its large size, thinly-spread population and the existence of a large French-speaking minority (historically about 25% of the population this century), Canada developed a federal system of government which made allowance for different regional and linguistic interests. These carry inherent tensions which have in recent years mostly concerned the political status of Quebec, the second largest and predominantly French-speaking province which witnessed a rise in nationalism in the 1960s.

The failure from the 1970s to early 1990s of attempted constitutional reforms aimed at helping

Quebec protect its language and culture gave rise to two "sovereignty" referendums which both however failed, the second in 1995 very narrowly. The 1990s has witnessed the birth of several regionally based parties replacing the traditional nation-wide parties. The Conservative government of the 1980s was left with only two seats in Parliament after the 1993 election.

They were replaced by the liberals (a Canada-wide party) led by Quebec politician Jean Chretien, whose government was re-elected for a third term of office following the Federal elections held in November 2000. Paul Martin's Liberal Party won a minority victory in the June 2004 general elections, but twelve years of Liberal government ended when he was defeated by Stephen Harper's opposition Conservatives in January 2006.

In 2008 Stephen Harper again went to the country and currently leads a minority government. Michael Ignatieff (liberal party) is the present leader of the opposition. The Head of State in Canada is Queen Elizabeth II, with Michaelle Jean as Governor General.

Chapter 16: Travel and Health Advice

The vast majority of British business visitors to Canada will arrive by air. There are direct flights from British airports to the Canadian gateways of Calgary, Edmonton, Halifax, Montreal, Ottawa, St John's, Toronto and Vancouver. Alternatively, a good proportion of flights come via US hubs such as New York, Chicago or San Francisco, to the same airports for roughly the same fare.

Toronto

Pearson International Airport (YYZ) is situated 24km north-west of downtown Toronto. There are bus services to the Yorkdale, York Mills and Islington subway stops which run every 20 minutes.

There are also shuttle buses from the airport to the major hotels taking around 60 minutes.

Halifax

The airport (YHZ) is situated 33 km from the city. There are no public buses to or from the airport. However, there are shuttle buses that run between the airport and downtown, which also stop at the major hotels. The journey takes around 45 minutes.

Montreal

Montreal is served by Dorval International Airport (YUL), 25 km from the city centre. The best way into town from Dorval is by bus or by one of the hotel courtesy buses. The trip takes around 30 minutes.

Calgary

Calgary is served by Calgary International Airport which is approximately 30 minutes from downtown. Calgary Transit provides public bus transportation to and from the airport via Route 57 with service to and from the Whitehorn LRT Station.

Ottawa

Ottawa is served by Macdonald-Cartier International Airport which is approximately 30 minutes from downtown. There are shuttle buses available and public transports.

Vancouver

Vancouver is served by Vancouver International Airport which is approximately 20 minutes from downtown. The Canada Line is a new rapid transit rail link connecting to downtown Vancouver in 26 minutes and to downtown Richmond in 18 minutes. You can conveniently gain access to trains from both the international and domestic terminals. There are also courtesy shuttles to many of the local hotels.

Passports/visas

British Citizens and British Overseas Citizens who are entitled to re-admission to the UK do not require a visa to enter Canada; neither do citizens of British dependent territories who derive their citizenship through birth, descent, registration or naturalisation in one of the British dependent territories of Anguilla, Bermuda, British Virgin Islands, Cayman Islands, Falkland Islands, Gibraltar, Montserrat, Pitcairn, St Helena, Turks & Caicos Islands.

For information on visas, see the Canada International Gateway website. Please be sure to check with the Canadian High Commission if you expect to remain for a lengthy period of time in Canada.

Health advice

There are no specific vaccinations recommended or required for a trip to Canada. It is advisable to be in date for tetanus, polio and diptheria. Rabies is present in more remote areas but is unlikely to pose a risk to business travellers.

Information on health hazards and precautions to take when travelling abroad can be found in the leaflet 'Health advice for travellers' available from main Post offices.

It is essential to take out full medical insurance when visiting Canada as there are no reciprocal healthcare agreements between Canada and the UK. Tap water in Canada is universally safe to drink.

Electricity

120-240V (mostly 120V) 60 cycles AC with two pin flat prong plug fittings (or three pin with one round and two flat prongs) and screw type lamp sockets. Adapters and transformers are available for appliances using other voltages.

The Canada Official Tourist website can assist you with planning your trip.

Chapter 17: Customs and Regulations

Most imports to Canada (except those of low pecuniary value) require a Canada customs invoice. Additional information is required for textiles. Copies of the prescribed forms can be obtained from certain commercial stationers.

Commercial shipments of relatively low pecuniary value may use an ordinary commercial invoice or other document in support of the declared value of goods. Specimen copies of the Canadian Customs invoices and bill of entry and other forms may be obtained from the Canadian High Commission. For up to date customs information for Canada please visit www.cbsa.ca Canada operates the World Customs Organisation's

Harmonised System (HS) nomenclature

Tariffs are levied on the free on board (fob) value of the goods in the country of export and may be specific or ad valorem. Special tariffs are in operation for Commonwealth countries (British Preferential schedule), USA and Mexico (NAFTA schedule) Israel and Chile. Most other countries are placed on the most-favoured-nation tariff. The remainder trade on a slightly higher general tariff schedule.

HM Revenue & Customs provides information and guides to assist you with the export process. The first line of enquiry for routine tariff classification advice down to the 6 digit Harmonised System subheading level, used worldwide is the National Advice Service (NAS).

Additional Taxes

Since 1 January 1991, imported goods have generally been subject to the federal VAT-style Goods and Services Tax (GST). The 5% GST, is payable on entry on the duty and excise-paid value of the goods.

For GST purposes a number of goods and services are zero-rates (these goods also do not attract GST upon import). They include most agricultural and fish products, certain major purchases by farmers and fishermen, basic groceries, prescribed medical devices and prescription drugs.

Legislation and Local Regulations

Inspection rules change frequently so exporters should check the requirements either with their customer or with the relevant pre-shipment company.

Labelling and Packaging Regulations

This is of particular importance to Canada as the country in officially bilingual. Under the Consumer Packaging and Labelling Act, special federal packaging and labelling requirements have to be met for pre-packaged food products and most consumer items exported to Canada. Bilingual labelling in English and French is required on all consumer products. The regulations provide for placement of identification data, identification of the manufacturer, product information and standard quality disclosures.

Additionally, many food products must also comply with strict hygiene and ingredients regulations. Some goods for personal or household use, hardware, novelties and sporting goods, paper products and clothes must be clearly marked, stamped, branded or labelled so as to indicate the country of origin.

In addition, any imported textile article must have a label affixed to it which states the textile fibre content of the article. Imported packages of tobacco, cigarettes and cigars also have special packaging and stamping requirements. For food products, the Food and Drugs Act Regulations stipulate which foods offered for sale must carry a label and also the required contents of the label. Strict requirements for pharmaceuticals also exist. Attractive packaging is essential in Canada.

Canadian law strictly regulates packaging, which must be manufactured, filed and displayed in such a manner that the consumer is not misled as to the quality or quantity of the product. Further information on the labelling of non-food products can be obtained from www.ic.gc.ca.

For Food products, see www.agr.gc.ca. The Liquor control Board of Ontario (LCBO) is Canada's largest alcohol retailer, has developed new standards for the shipping of Tetra Pak containers to ensure proper handling at every stage in the supply chain. For detailed information, visit www.lcbotrade.com. The

Canadian Food Inspection Agency (CFIA) has approved the adoption of an international measure to prevent the introduction of foreign pests through wooden packaging materials. Exemptions will be made for wood packaging originating from the continental United States.

Certain other packaging products may also be exempt depending on the type, thickness or origin of the wood being used.

Export Controls and Licensing

The UK Government maintains export controls on a range of goods such as arts and antiques, Medicines and prescription drugs, chemicals, food, animals, plants and horticulture and strategic goods (including military goods, software, technology and so called dual-use items). If items are subject to UK export controls, a license is required before they can be exported by any Means. Dependent on the nature of your goods, different government departments are responsible for issuing licences. Dependent on the export destination, sanctions and embargoes might also apply. The export of most goods from the UK to Canada is unrestricted. Some items including arms, explosives, military equipment, atomic energy equipment, metals and minerals, antiques, works of art, diamonds, computer technology and live animals are subject to control, although sometimes temporarily.

Standards and technical regulation

The British Standards Institution (BSI) can provide information and advice on compliance with overseas statutory and other technical requirements through their Professional Services team. BSI can supply detailed information on foreign regulations; identify, supply and assist in the Interpretation of foreign standards and approval procedures; research and consult on technical requirements for a specific product; and provide translations of foreign standards, items of legislation and codes of practice. Fees vary according to the amount of work involved. For further information visit the BSI website.

The UK National Physical Laboratory maintains detailed information on international aspects of standards, accreditation and measurement infrastructure, including more specific facts and figures for a number of countries. The information should help exporters and investors form a view of a country's underpinning technological infrastructure, vital to trade and product quality.

Intellectual Property Rights

Advice on matters relating to patents, designs or trade markets can be obtained from agents specialising in these fields. Names and addresses of these are provided at a small charge by the Chartered Institute of Patent Agents. The Patent Act and Regulations define the procedures for obtaining and enforcing patent rights in Canada.

Application to register a patent should be made to: Canadian Intellectual Property Office (CIPO) Place du Portage 50 Victoria St., Room C-229 Gatineau, Quebec K1A 0C9 For international callers: Telephone: General enquiries: 819-934-0544 Fax: Enquiries only: 819-953-7620 Submit IP documents: 819-953-CIPO (2476) Business Hours 8:30 a.m. to 5:00 p.m. (ET) Monday to Friday The first inventor to file a patent application for an invention is entitled to a patent for that invention.

It usually takes three years from the filing of the application to the granting of a patent. Patents are granted in Canada for 20 years from the date of application. On expiry, patented inventions become public property and renewal is unavailable.

Registration of a trademark grants the owner the exclusive right to use that trade mark throughout Canada. Trademarks are protected for 15 years from the date of registration and are renewable for 15 year periods without limitation. IP rights are territorial, that is they only give protection in the countries where they are granted or registered. If you are thinking about trading internationally then you should consider registering your IP rights abroad.

Chapter 18: Conclusion

Language

In Canada the official languages spoken are English and French. Most native French speakers in Canada live in the province of Quebec and interpretation may be required for business meetings.

All laws of the federal government are enacted in both English and French and that federal government services must be available in both languages. The National Centre for Languages can assist with language training, interpreting and translation services.

Meetings, Negotiations and Presentations

It is important to be on time and appropriately dressed for the venue you are holding the meeting. Face to face meetings are important and this will be the opportunity to build up a rapport immediately which will help with negotiations and discussions. Presentations should be well prepared, clear and be thorough in your knowledge.

Hours of business

Working hours vary throughout the country. Some small businesses close completely in July and August and government departments may work variable hours during the summer months. Fewer UK business visitors come to Canada during the winter months of December-March.

- Government and Business: 08.30 - 17.00, Monday to Friday.
- Banking: 10.00-17:00 Monday to Thursday, 10.00-18.00 Friday. Some banks in large centres operate much longer hours including evenings, and Saturdays.
- Shops: There is a five-day working week, but most retails stores in cities open on Saturday and often on Sunday as well. Late shopping (to 21.00) on Thursday or Friday is common in large cities; in suburban shopping centres, supermarkets often stay open until 21.00 or 22.00 (Monday to Friday). Some convenience stores and supermarkets remain open 24 hours a day, especially in heavily populated areas.
- Lunch and dinner meetings: Canadians do conduct business over meals but tend to eat early, 12.00 for lunches and 6.30pm-7.00pm for dinners.

What are the challenges?

Canada is a relatively straightforward market to work in; however, the importance of relationship building should not be underestimated even though Canadians are relaxed and approachable in their business dealings. Canada is a foreign market with business differences in comparison both to the UK and USA. Companies should always consider legal advice if they are unsure about any formal agreements.

Food and drink products

All meat and meat by products from the UK are banned from entry into Canada. Dairy products are subject to an import quota system (between the EU and Canada): see the Canadian Food Inspection Agency website. Alcoholic beverages are purchased and sold through the Canadian Provincial Governments (with the exception of Alberta).

How to Invest in Canada

First contact should be with the Federal Government via Canadian representatives at the Canadian High commission in London. Please visit the website www.tradecommissioner.gc.ca or you can visit the website www.investincanada.gc.ca which highlights specific regions and relevant information for British Columbia, Alberta, Nova Scotia, and Quebec.

Secondly you can also obtain information via the Provincial Economic Development Ministries: www.investinontario.com   www.ontariocanada.com www.mdeie.gouv.qc.ca   (Quebec)   www.alberta-canada.com (Alberta) www.investbc.com (British Columbia) www.gov.ns.ca/econ (Nova Scotia)

Good Luck!